HOUGHTON MIFFLIN
Reading
A Legacy of Literacy

That's Amazing!

HOUGHTON MIFFLIN   BOSTON · MORRIS PLAINS, NJ

California · Colorado · Georgia · Illinois · New Jersey · Texas

Design, Art Management and Page Production: Kirchoff/Wohlberg, Inc.

ILLUSTRATION CREDITS
4-21 Kyrsten Brooker. **22-39** Kristen Bennett Chavez. **40-57** Terry Widener.

Printed in U.S.A.

ISBN: 0-618-04400-0

6789-VH-05 04 03 02

That's Amazing!

Contents

ONE DAY IN MAY

by **Kitty Colton**
illustrated by **Kyrsten Brooker**

Strategy Focus

Spring is supposed to bring sunshine and beautiful colors. But all Lin sees is gray, gray, gray! As you read, **monito**r how well you're following the story events.

Spring had come to the city. At least the calendar said so. There it was, in big, bold letters: May.

But when Lin looked out her window, everything looked gray.

She saw no trees bursting with pale green buds.
No candy-colored flowers poking through the
ground. No bluebirds carrying twigs and leaves to
line their nests. Not even a black-and-yellow bee.

All she saw was gray. Gray walls and gray
roofs. Gray streets and gray steam rising from the
grates. A patch of gray sky between the tall gray
buildings.

She went outside, sat on her gray stoop, and sighed. She thought about spring at her old home, in the country. "I wish we'd never moved to the city," she said to her gray cat, Cleo.

A fat tear rolled down Lin's cheek. Cleo leaped off the stoop to chase a pigeon.

"My my, you look like a storm cloud," said a sunny voice. Lin looked up, startled. A woman was sitting on the tree stump in front of her building.

"Huh?" Lin said, wiping her eyes. The city was crowded with people. But she had never seen anyone like this.

The woman's eyes gleamed like pieces of blue
sea glass. Her hair was piled up like a bird's nest,
woven with twigs and leaves. Her skirt was a deep
velvety green, soft as the mossy floor of the forest.

Cleo stopped chasing the pigeon and stared.
(Being a cat, she didn't care about being rude.)
Then, to Lin's horror, Cleo jumped straight onto the
woman's head.

"Oh!" Lin cried out, laughing. "I'm sorry. Cleo, you get down from there, you bad cat." But Cleo was already half buried in the woman's tangled mass of hair.

"No, that's purrrrr-fectly fine," the woman replied calmly, as if animals jumped into her hair all day long.

Lin remembered that she was in a very bad mood. She started to scowl again.

"Tell me what's troubling you on such a lovely day," the woman said. Just then, the pigeon landed on her shoulder. "Helloooo!" she cooed at it.

"It's not a lovely day at all!" Lin said. "I hate the city. Back where I used to live, spring meant flowers and birds and blue sky. Here everything is just gray and dead."

The pigeon squawked loudly. "He says, 'What's wrong with gray?'" the woman told Lin. Cleo poked her head out and meowed her agreement.

Lin shrugged and kicked at the stump.

"You shouldn't kick trees," the woman said gently. "They have feelings too, you know."

"But it's just a dead stump!" Lin said, and she kicked it again because that was the mood she was in.

The woman jumped to her feet and pointed down. A branch had sprouted up where she was sitting.

"Sometimes you don't notice what's right in front of your nose," she said.

15

Lin folded her arms stubbornly.

"Or what's right outside your window," the woman added. She pointed to a pile of gray twigs perched on Lin's building.

Lin heard a faint chirp, chirp. Suddenly a large bird swooped down to the ledge, and the chirps grew louder. "A nest of baby falcons," the woman said. Cleo's eyes grew round as moons.

"Nature isn't just bright colors," said the woman. "Gray has its place too. Without gray skies and rain, there would be no flowers. And no worms to feed the baby birds."

17

She paused and then added, half to herself, "But maybe there *has* been too much rain lately."

Just then, a bright burst of sun made Lin shade her eyes. Neighbors appeared on their stoops. They smiled and lifted their heads to the warmth, contented as Cleo.

"It really is spring!" Lin said. She ran up the stairs and into her house. She grabbed her brother, who was in front of his computer, as always.

"But I don't want to go outside!" he cried as they reached the doorway. "It's just a dumb old gray—"

19

The streets were soaked with sunshine. The city was bursting with the colors and sounds of spring.

Lin looked for her new friend, but she was gone. A patch of pink tulips had sprouted in her place. Cleo lay beside them, licking her sun-warmed fur.

Responding

1 What color is Cleo the cat?

2 Why do you think the woman says the gray day is lovely?

3 What details show that the woman is unusual?

NOTING DETAILS

One way to understand how details are used by an author is to make a web. Copy the web on a piece of paper and write in details that the author uses to show how gray the setting is.

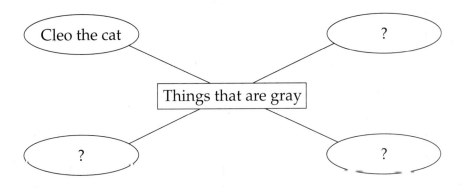

21

Tattercoat

A Cinderella Tale from England

retold by
Susan Delaney

illustrated by
Kristen Bennett
Chavez

Strategy Focus

Tattercoat's life gets off to a sad start. As you read, think of **questions** to ask about the lesson of the story.

I once knew a family whose house was filled with laughter and song. Their happiness spread like sunshine over the surrounding hills.

Then things changed, as things often do.

The daughter grew up and married a young lord from a nearby village.

A year later, the couple had a baby girl. But just after the child was born, the daughter died. The family's joy died that day as well.

Soon after, the young lord was called away to battle. He wept as he kissed his baby goodbye. But part of him was glad to go to war. Perhaps on the battlefield he could forget his sadness. The baby was left in her grandparents' care.

But the grandparents wanted nothing to do with the baby. When they looked into her blue eyes, they saw only their lost daughter. They had no room in their hearts for love.

When the child was older, the grandparents put her in their servants' care. But the servants had children of their own, and no time or love to give to another. So they treated the child badly.

The servants called her Tattercoat,
because the coat she wore was torn and
ragged. She lived on crusts of bread and rinds
of cheese. She slept in the dampest, coldest
corner of the house.

The girl accepted all this with good grace. She quietly did whatever the servants told her to, and she never complained.

But when evening came, Tattercoat spent hours wandering the hills behind the house. That's when I first heard her sobbing.

And that's when I became Tattercoat's
one true friend.

Time passed, and Tattercoat grew into a graceful young woman.

On the day the king was to give a ball, she told me, "Oh, I wish we could go. I imagine a ball is like the music from your flute, beautiful and magical all at once."

"Perhaps if we stand outside the castle, we can hear the music drift through the windows," I said. Tattercoat's face lit up with excitement. So we began the long walk to the palace.

    As we walked, a young man on a gray
horse came up beside us. "Do you mind
some company?" he asked. "I've been
traveling a long way by myself."

    The stranger and Tattercoat talked and
laughed all the way to the castle. I had never
seen her look so happy. I lagged behind,
playing a tune on my flute.

When we neared the castle, the young
man turned to Tattercoat. "Do you know who
I am?" he asked.

"No sir, I'm sorry. Should I know you?"
answered Tattercoat.

"I am the king's son," he said. "I'm on my way to my father's ball. Won't you please come as my guest? I must see you again." Tattercoat's eyes shone with joy. She nodded her head shyly.

The prince galloped off on his horse, shouting back, "Until tonight!"

When the prince was gone, Tattercoat looked down at her clothes with a frown. "How could a prince ever care for a poor girl in rags?" she asked me.

But I knew that whoever fell in love with Tattercoat while my flute sang its magic did not see the rags she wore. Instead, he saw the goodness in her heart.

Before the ball, Tattercoat rested beneath a tall tree. I began to play my magic flute again as she drifted off to sleep. When she woke up, Tattercoat looked like a princess. Her rags had changed to a deep blue gown, and on her once-bare feet were sparkling silver shoes. She blinked as she looked at herself.

"Am I dreaming?" she asked, turning to me.

"No," I said. "You just woke up from a long nightmare."

When we arrived at the ball, the prince took Tattercoat's hand and led her to the king and queen. "Father and Mother," he began, "this is Tattercoat. Nowhere is there a kinder or more loving girl. If she will have me, I wish to marry her."

Tattercoat and the Prince danced joyfully all night. Soon after, they were married.

Did they live happily ever after?
Of course. I wouldn't have it any other way.

Responding

Think About the Selection

1. Who tells the story?

2. Why is Tattercoat treated so badly?

3. Compare Tattercoat's life before she meets the prince and her life after she meets him.

Compare and Contrast

Copy the chart on a piece of paper. Then check whether parts of *Cinderella* are the same as *Tattercoat* or different.

Cinderella	Same as Tattercoat	Different from Tattercoat
Cinderella wears dirty rags.	✔	
Cinderella is dressed up like a princess.	?	?
Cinderella has a fairy godmother.	?	?
Cinderella and the prince marry.	?	?

THE BIG GUST

by Andrew Clements
illustrated by Terry Widener

Strategy Focus

Some strange things happen in this story. As you read, stop once in a while to **evaluate** how the author tells you this story is a fantasy.

It was just another day in Mayville. Folks were doing the things that they did in the summer. And then that one big gust came through.

Everyone in Mayville knows where they were at the time.

Jean Adams had a dog named Clipper. Jean often said, "That name is perfect for my dog. I always have to clip her hair and nails."

When the big gust came, in fact, Clipper was getting clipped. She was also yawning. The wind blew into her mouth.

Clipper blew up until she was ten times bigger than before. Then away she went. Jean went after her.

It wasn't long before the police got a call. "Help! I'm being chased by a barking balloon with hair ribbons!" yelled the caller.

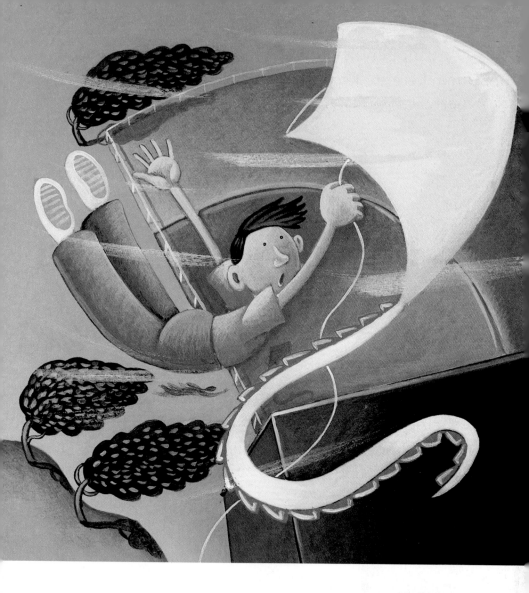

Tommy James was flying his new kite at the ball field. When the big gust came, Tommy held on tight. He went on a wild kite ride to the schoolyard.

Tommy saw the flagpole. He looped his legs and then the string around it. Then he slid down to the ground. He was safe and sound, but he had to leave the kite behind.

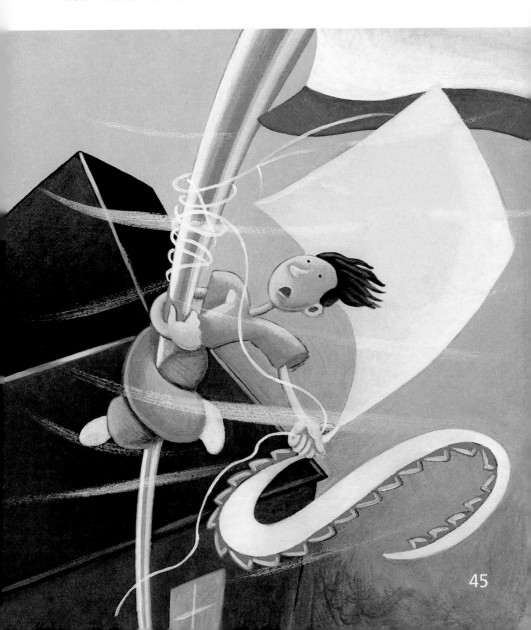

Elsie Chen was watering her garden. When the big gust came, it swept the hat off her head. Elsie turned around to see where her hat went.

When she turned back, her garden was on the roof of the house next door.

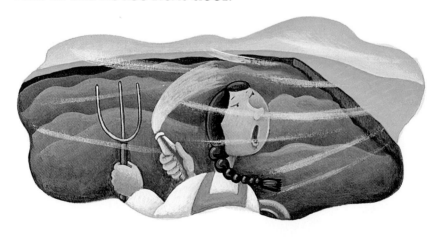

"Oh, good," thought Elsie. "Now my tomatoes are closer to the sun. I'll just get a longer hose and a tall ladder from the hardware store. I wonder if my neighbors will mind."

They didn't. Elsie's tomatoes got a lot of sunshine, water, and special attention up on that roof. Then they won first prize at the county fair!

At the school gym, some kids were playing kickball. When the big gust came, the doors flew open. You'll never guess what blew in. It was a pond, with three ducks, six lily pads, three frogs, and one tall man in a little red rowboat!

The tall man stayed to play water polo with the kids. The ducks and frogs watched the game from the red rowboat. The lily pads just sat there, taking up space.

Bob Belcher was mowing his lawn. When the big gust came, Bob and his mower took off like a driver and a racing car.

Together they cut a path through six front yards and a blackberry thicket.

The big gust blew all the grass Bob mowed to the town library. It formed a pile on the front steps. Soon a bunch of kids were reading their books on that soft, delicious-smelling green carpet.

   Over at the Sport Shop, Jane Asher was
putting some tennis balls on the shelf. When the
big gust came, they blew off the shelf and then blew
all the way to Chestertown, along with other balls
of all shapes and sizes.

That afternoon there was a news flash from
Chestertown. "Tim Lewis here in the middle of a
hailstorm. Some hailstones are as big as tennis
balls. I mean softballs. No, wait a minute. . . .
footballs! Could they be as big as bowling balls?
Oh no, BASKETBALLS! HELP!"

Gary Jones was all set to fix his picket fence. When the big gust came, every single picket and a whole box of nails went up in a jumble. But when they came down, Gary had a new fence. And he'd never even picked up his hammer!

After that, Gary tried to build fences by juggling pickets, nails, and his hammer. As you might guess, he became a better juggler than a fence builder. So he joined the circus when it came to town.

55

As fast as it came, the big gust left town. But the folks in Mayville will never forget that windy day.

Strange things have happened since then. But nothing has been as wild as that one big gust!

Responding

Think About the Selection

1 Who is watering her garden when the big gust comes?

2 What does the caller tell the police?

3 What is the barking balloon, really? How does she get that way?

Fantasy/Realism

Copy this chart on a piece of paper. Then write things from the story that could really happen and things that could not.

What Could Happen	What Could Not Happen
Wind blows a kite through the air.	Wind blows a boy holding a kite through the air.
?	?
?	?